What Parents Need to Know about Teens

FACTS, MYTHS AND STRATEGIES

David A. Wolfe

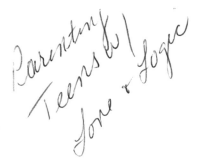

camh

Centre for Addiction and Mental Health
Centre de toxicomanie et de santé mentale

Library and Archives Canada Cataloguing in Publication

Wolfe, David A.
　What Parents Need to Know about Teens : facts, myths and strategies / David A. Wolfe.

　1. Parent and teenager. 2. Parenting. 3. Teenagers.
I. Centre for Addiction and Mental Health II. Title.

HQ799.15.W64 2007　　　　649'.125　　C2007-904093-4

ISBN: 978-0-88868-604-6 (PRINT)
ISBN: 978-0-88868-605-3 (PDF)
ISBN: 978-0-88868-606-0 (HTML)

Printed in Canada

For information on other CAMH publications or to place an order, please contact:
Sales and Distribution
Tel.: 1 800 661-1111 or 416 595-6059 in Toronto
E-mail: publications@camh.net
Website: www.camh.net

Disponible en français sous le titre *Ce que les parents doivent savoir sur leurs adolescents : Faits, mythes et stratégies*

This book was produced by:
Development: Margaret Kittel Canale, CAMH
Editorial: Jacquelyn Waller-Vintar, CAMH; Deborah Viets; Deborah England
Design: Nancy Leung, CAMH
Typesetting: BTT Communications
Print production: Christine Harris, CAMH

3517a / 10-07 PM065

Contents

What this booklet is about

You've probably picked up this booklet because you want practical, accurate and user-friendly information to help you raise your teen. You want to know what's considered normal adolescent behaviour, how to determine whether your child is on a good path, how to encourage his healthy development and how to get help when problems arise. There are many new things influencing teens today, but your parenting role is as important today as ever before. Spending time strengthening your relationship with your teen is the best investment in her future, just as it was when she was a child.

In my work with adolescents, I'm often asked by parents, "What do I need to know to help my teen avoid alcohol and other drugs, abusive peers or dating partners and other worries?" News reports are filled with upsetting stories about injuries and other forms of harm stemming from drinking, driving, partying or bullying—which makes parents all the more concerned. Today's pressures on teens come in different forms than in previous generations, but pressure is pressure, and to a teen it can seem overwhelming at times.

Parents may also feel overwhelmed with the problems and situations teens bring home, especially when some of these didn't exist when they were growing up, like Internet bullying or chat rooms. Many parents feel they would benefit from advice about how to meet their teens' needs, how to promote maturity and responsibility, and ways to avoid danger.

It's true that adolescence is the most dangerous period of development, especially from ages 16 to 19, and even extending to age 24, when many finish their college or university studies and save a bit of money before leaving (or being gently nudged from) the family nest. After age 16, the combination of greater access to adult privileges such as driving, extended curfews, alcohol and other drugs, empty family homes or even separate living arrangements makes this age ripe for trouble. But, the image of teens as immature, fun seeking and irresponsible is overblown and inaccurate. The vast majority of teens emerge from this period unscathed—especially when their parents or caregivers practise effective parenting and do their utmost to prepare, not scare, their teen for assuming these new responsibilities and the pressures that may accompany them.

As parents, we know that simply letting our teenagers learn for themselves is not a good choice. The risk of injury or long-term health problems that could result is too high. Likewise, simply telling teens they can't do certain things ("Just say no!") doesn't work. Threatening them with consequences ("If I catch you drinking, you'll be grounded for a month!"), or putting up legal, or family, roadblocks to curtail activities are not very effective with teens. We need to help them develop personal strategies, a sense of responsibility, and values that reduce their chances of harm, especially now that they are spending much more time doing things on their own.

We can choose to sit and wait for our teenagers to make mistakes and react to them—usually through punishments or lectures—or we can try to head off problems by being a reliable source of information and support. While we can't make all the choices for them, we can assist them in making the most responsible choices possible. The best way to achieve this goal is to maintain a balance between being sensitive to their desires and needs, yet firm in providing guidance and direction.

Keep in mind that adolescence is all about *experimentation*. Because a certain amount of experimentation is normal, our job as parents is to figure out how to strike a balance between setting limits (yes—teens need limits) and promoting their independence (yes—teens need to develop their *own* limits). This balancing act between hanging on and letting go is a major challenge of parenting a teenager.

As the parent of a teen you need information about three key issues:

- You need information about what behaviour is "normal" during adolescence so that you can better understand and guide your teen. Because none of us is born an expert parent, you probably worked hard to understand your child during infancy and early childhood. Adolescence requires the same amount of effort—if not more!
- You need a basic understanding of how you and your family, in addition to your teen, are changing. By recognizing the challenges that you and your teen face during this time of rapid transition, you will be better prepared to be a source of strength and guidance.
- Finally, you need information on the best ways to be an effective parent during this period of development so that you are strengthening your relationship with your teen and avoiding some of the common "traps."

The purpose of this booklet is to help you get a better understanding of these key issues pertaining to adolescent development, and how your role as a parent can make an important difference in how teens develop the ability to make good choices. In three future booklets, we will discuss topics of specific concern in greater depth—topics such as substance use, peer and dating relationships, Internet use and adolescent well-being.

How teens manage their relationships—with family members, with peers and with other important adults—is a key element in how they learn to make safe and responsible choices. Ultimately, the process begins with their relationship with you. Now as much as ever, what parents do *does* matter.

Strategies for effective parenting

BEING AN EFFECTIVE PARENT TAKES PLANNING

Let's begin by looking at some typical situations faced by Canadian families:

Mike and Wendy, *both in their late 30s, have three children, two careers, a nice house in a great location with friendly neighbours—and a problem. Their 14-year-old son, Jeremy, has been worrying them a lot lately. Ever since he started Grade 9, the "old Jeremy"—the fun-loving, average school kid who won soccer medals, played in the band, and collected comics and Space Lego—seems to have vanished. Now he spends his time either out or online with his new (and gruff) friends from high school, while his homework piles up and his grades drop. Any conversation he has with his parents rapidly turns into an argument, and the more Mike and Wendy try to get him to abide by the rules, the more surly and upset he becomes. They aren't disagreeable parents, but they want him to see things their way. Is it wrong for them to make sure he eats and sleeps properly, gets good grades at school and doesn't get into trouble? Why does Jeremy make everything so difficult?*

Miranda *experiences some of the same problems with her daughter Stephanie. As a single mom, Miranda has to carefully juggle her time between her job and her two children—and Stephanie seems to be using* *up more than her share of her mother's energy. Stephanie's room's a mess, she's never around when important chores have to be done, she spends most evenings either online with friends or on the cellphone—the list goes on. Miranda is torn between allowing her daughter enough freedom to go out with her friends and have some fun, and making her face up to her responsibilities around the house. Recently, Stephanie has been dating a boy a year older than her, and Miranda's worried about how far she can be trusted with evenings out, parties and all of the other distractions and worries that dating creates. Like Jeremy, Stephanie doesn't seem to be too focused on schoolwork, or on the other things that used to take up her time, such as choir and skating. What should Miranda do to supervise her daughter without stifling her at the same time?*

Fatim and Harshil *have a different sort of difficulty. Since moving to Canada five years ago, they have watched their eldest daughter, Noor, adapt to the new society around them. Already, she is much more comfortable speaking English than they are, and she has gradually adjusted to social customs that her grandparents would never have condoned. Fatim especially wants Noor to be more respectful of their family traditions and customs, but Noor seems more interested in her friends—their clothes, parties, music, makeup and language—than in any of the values her parents hold. She argues that she is kept at home while her friends are allowed all kinds of freedoms, and complains that her parents are being unfair. While Fatim and Harshil are pleased that they have found a home where their daughter is relatively safe and able to express herself, they* *worry their values are being lost. They are afraid if she is allowed all of the liberties that Canadian teens are permitted, Noor will abandon those things that her parents worked so hard to preserve. How can Fatim and Harshil give Noor what she wants without sacrificing the customs and traditions they value?*

Do any of these situations sound familiar? If you are the parent of a teenager (or guardian, grandparent, aunt, uncle, even a friend of a teenager) I'm sure that you will run into situations similar to these. Although the problems and conflicts may sound familiar, the approaches and solutions to them often aren't.

The families just discussed are facing changes that occur rapidly as their teens begin the task of seeking their own identity and gradually separating from their role as children in the family. The teens have no particular roadmap or guide to follow, but they're caught up in a fast-moving adventure driven by their peer culture, curiosity and new-found opportunities. Limit-testing, mood changes and sharply critical attitudes may come with this territory, but your values, your role modelling, your affection and your time and guidance deeply influence the decisions and actions they take. Focus on the bigger picture (your teen's maturity and independence), and accept that getting there is not always easy.

As parents, we're bombarded with advice, warnings and criticism concerning parenting. However, we seldom have the opportunity to think about how we raise our teens. We most often rely on the same familiar methods our own parents used (even if we have bad memories of them) simply because there is so much information out there—talk shows, countless parenting magazines at the grocery checkout, more Internet sites than any parent could ever look at, parent chat rooms and bulletin boards—but no way to know what or who we can trust. Sometimes we hold our breath and wait to see if anything "bad" happens and then react, rather than spending a little time thinking about our role and planning ways to handle tricky situations with our teens.

Your teenager's new connections with friends pose new challenges to your relationship. Although peers can and do influence one another in positive ways, we also know that they increase the likelihood your teen will experiment with tobacco, alcohol, other drugs, unsafe sex and delinquent behaviour. You are now confronted with an entirely new set of worries and concerns.

Although this may sound bleak, parents do continue to influence the behaviours and decisions of their children well into and beyond the teen years in extremely important ways. Your relationship is changing for sure, but this process does not have to be painful or unpleasant—in fact, the changes you are both undergoing are some of the most important, valuable and long-lasting of all.

KEEPING UP WITH YOUR TEEN

The idea for this guide arose from my experience and that of my colleagues in listening to adolescents as part of our efforts to provide educational strategies to strengthen their healthy relationships and reduce risk behaviours. Simply stated, teens are eager for guidance about the best ways to fit in with their peers—both same-sex and opposite-sex peers—without making mistakes that can get them into trouble or lead to rejection. They are also eager for information about the choices they have concerning new pressures and expectations (such as sex, substance use, and avoiding abuse from peers or dating partners). However, they must trust the source of the information, feel they are being heard, know their opinions are respected, and have some degree of say in their decisions. In other words, they do not like to simply be told "just say no" or "because I say so."

Teens often express the wish their parents would make more of an effort to understand the challenges and pressures they face at school, at home and in the community. During classroom discussions about these pressures, I often hear them say "My parents need to know this!" They voice concern that their parents are quick with the rules and consequences of breaking them, but don't seem to take the time to really listen and help to problem-solve the situations that matter to their teen (for example, working together on the answer to "Can I go to a party Friday night?"). Worse, they may feel that their parents hold outdated views from their own teenaged years, or that they rely on newspaper headlines of tragedies, leading them to make unbalanced and unfair decisions. I'm not saying they're right—I just want you to remember where they're coming from!

To get around these concerns, some teens find it easier to create a "parent-persona" in order to avoid suspicion and appear to be the same kid their parent has always known. By keeping their new-found interests, friends and opportunities secret, they believe they can get away with more things and at the same time, keep their parents happy.

A teen who takes the parent-persona route, for example, may know that his parent will be concerned about his going to a party, so he will head this off with a prepared statement such as "Pat's parents will be there. There's no booze or drugs— I don't do that. You can trust me—there's no need to phone Pat's parents." This approach stems from the time-honoured adage, "the less they know the better," and, to an unsuspecting parent, this may lessen his worry and help maintain the perception that his teen is more trustworthy and mature than the rest (until the inevitable happens).

Other teens are more upfront and confrontational, choosing to simply override parental authority and launch into their new-found status and privileges with abandon. A "so what?" or "who cares?" attitude can elevate their status among peers and force a new relationship onto their parents. These teens are more likely to be the "early starters," leading the way as they and their friends try out new temptations such as substance use, romantic relationships and sexual activity.

Being this type of "leader" during early adolescence, of course, carries many risks. Not only are there risks directly related to these activities (for example, pregnancy, sexually transmitted infections, injuries and addictions), but there are indirect risks as well (for example, academic decline, violence, bullying and delinquent activities) that some teens will entirely ignore or minimize, focusing instead on the elevated status they gain from their peers.

You know your child best. You know that there is no magic pill, no simple method that works every time, and mistakes do happen. You've been learning the best ways to raise her all along. Now you just need to continue learning: What's normal? What's changing? What role do you play during this time? Although it's seldom easy, there are some simple strategies that should guide you as you navigate new issues. This booklet tackles these issues from the perspective of *normal adolescent development,* and it draws from research studies and the author's experience raising teens to provide practical advice for strengthening your relationship with your teen and minimizing conflict.

The information is intended to make you think about, and perhaps change, some of the strategies you use as the parent of a teen—much as we ask teens to think about and revise their strategies for making safe and healthy decisions. There are no easy solutions or quick fixes, but there are some simple strategies that work better than others to foster the values and sense of responsibility you hope your teen will adopt. Being informed, and somewhat open-minded, is a great starting point.

Be an effective parent:
Balance sensitivity and firmness

Let's begin with a brief look at some essential things your teens need from you:

1 • They need information about the choices, responsibilities and consequences (limits + conseq)
that go along with the new opportunities and pressures they will face.

2 • They need to be prepared, not scared, to handle the pressures of adolescence.

3 • They need to feel that they can rely on you for understanding, support,
information and guidance (even if it means setting firm limits).

4 • They need you to show them positive ways to handle conflicts, disappointments,
risks and pressures from others, including you.

5 • They need to feel connected not only to friends but to school, family and
community. They also need to feel appreciated.

6 • They need to be seen as people (rather than as potential problems) and
treated fairly.

7 • They need guidance in problem-solving and decision-making so they can
think for themselves and be involved in their own solutions.

Perhaps most of all, during this short but critical time of adolescence, your
teen needs you to balance *sensitivity* toward the challenges and pressures she faces,
with the right amount of *firmness* to ensure that she paces herself and doesn't
assume that "anything goes." In other words, as a parent you have the task of
being both attentive and understanding, while at the same time stating clear

expectations and setting firm limits. Have a look at the next section, entitled "Examples of Parenting Styles," to see if you can recognize yourself, and to see if you are using the most effective strategies to parent your teen.

EXAMPLES OF PARENTING STYLES

THE ENFORCER (AUTHORITARIAN PARENT)

Some of us act like enforcers or guards when interacting with our teen. This means that we do not allow our teen to take part in any activity or gathering that we are not monitoring ourselves. We assume that teens must be watched constantly, and we forbid them to undertake any questionable activity. There are clear rules in place and punishments for breaking them, and we show little flexibility when it comes to complying with our wishes and demands. We believe we can eliminate potential problems through strict rules and discipline.

RESULT: The Enforcer shows little sensitivity for the pressures faced by young people, including their growing need for autonomy. Parents who take this strict approach soon lose the connection they have with their teenager. Young persons will not provide information that they think will be used against them. Instead they will resort to secrecy and keep their true motivations hidden. It is likely that teens who are confronted with this style of parenting will rebel against the unreasonable or rigid demands placed on them. Enforcers are quick to view the way they were brought up as the correct way to raise a teen.

THE FRIEND (PERMISSIVE PARENT)

Some of us are too easygoing, distant or out of touch and believe our teen is old enough to make his own choices and decisions. We believe that problems can occur regardless of what we do or say, so we might as well save ourselves the grief of arguing. Besides, we tell ourselves, how will our teenagers ever learn if we don't let them make decisions for themselves? We feel that teens learn important lessons by experiencing the natural conse-quences of the choices they make. We say to ourselves, "I did such and such when I was a kid, and it didn't hurt me."

RESULT: The Friend leaves too much to chance. These parents are not pro-viding the guidance or direction that a young person requires—teens need adult role models! Teenagers desperately want information and guidance during these difficult years, and they assume (usually without asking) that their parents will provide direction as needed. The chance that teenagers will develop serious problems increases greatly when parents are not involved in their decision making.

THE EFFECTIVE PARENT (AUTHORITATIVE PARENT)

Neither The Enforcer nor The Friend is using effective parenting, because they do not balance sensitivity and firmness. However, The Effective Parent knows that most teenagers today benefit from open discussions about the pressures and choices they face. We cultivate a caring, trusting relationship with our teens, but we are not afraid to be firm when circumstances demand it. Whenever possible, we provide up-to-date information, and we offer advice based on knowledge of our children and understanding of the potential harm that may come from risky activities, rather than resorting to scare tactics and threats. We do not always say no, nor do we always say yes. We carefully consider each activity or request, and then make a decision. As authoritative parents, we recognize the importance of consistency and clearly conveying our expectations.

RESULT: The Effective Parent has adapted to the changes that must occur as the young person moves from childhood to adolescence and the teen years. These parents know that these are difficult times for their teen, and they work to meet the social and emotional needs of the young person, while helping to limit the risks that will be taken. These parents and teens talk to each other regularly, discuss things openly and respect each other's point of view. When an unpopular decision needs to be made, effective parents are strong enough to do it. They may not always agree with, or get along with, their teen, but effective parents and the teenagers they assist work together to make good choices.

Balancing sensitivity and firmness is not as easy as it sounds (you've probably figured this out already). Each situation you and your teen face requires additional consideration on your part because there are few hard and fast rules. However, there are effective strategies. If you grasp this basic principle and approach each new situation with sensitivity and firmness in mind, the job will become easier for both of you. Effective parents make a conscious effort to understand the world of their adolescent, and they allow their teen to develop a sense of mastery over time.

Central to effective parenting is the vital role of relationships, both past and future. Healthy relationships do not come about by chance; they must be actively developed. The traditional view that teens present a host of problems fails to take into account the importance of developing relationships in a way that promotes positive communication and problem solving.

Adolescents who have had close relationships with parents, teachers, coaches and friends in the past are more likely to have a strong base from which to develop future relationships and resolve disagreements. Before we discuss ways in which you can help build these healthy relationships by practising effective parenting, consider the following dialogues:

COMMON DIALOGUES BETWEEN PARENTS AND TEENS

What style of parenting do you use—are you The Enforcer (authoritarian), The Friend (permissive) or The Effective Parent (authoritative and balanced)? In the dialogues below, see which response sounds most like yours would be if your teen approached you with the same request.

Teen: *"I'm going out with my friends now. See you later."*

THE ENFORCER (AUTHORITARIAN PARENT)

"You aren't going anywhere. I don't like your friends: they always seem to be getting into trouble. You need to stay in and get your homework done. Your last report card wasn't good enough."

RESULT: Your teenager feels that you don't trust him to make responsible choices and that you don't understand his need to be with his friends. He may begin to resent your authority and to resist your demands. Next time he may try to deceive you about what he is doing.

THE FRIEND (PERMISSIVE PARENT)

"See you later. I plan to go to bed early tonight. Be quiet when you come in."

RESULT: Your teenager can go wherever he wants and do whatever he wants. No one will check up on him. He will have to use his own judgment rather than guidance from you when he is faced with difficult choices. This will promote risky behaviour.

THE EFFECTIVE PARENT (AUTHORITATIVE PARENT)

"Wait a minute. First fill me in on where you'll be and who will be there. Do you need a ride? What do you plan to do? When will you be home? Call me if your plans change, please. Don't forget that you need to be home by midnight. I'll see you then. Have fun."

RESULT: Your teenager knows that you are paying attention and that you need to make sure that his plans are within reason. He may not like all the questions, but he knows that he is accountable to you for his whereabouts and his activities. If he knows he will be asked these questions each time he goes out, he can decide for himself whether or not the plans he makes with friends are a good idea. He also has a clear idea of what activities are acceptable to you, as you will give feedback on his responses to your questions. You and he are building a trusting relationship.

> **Teen:** *"Jane is having a sleepover at her house on Friday night. Can I go?"*

THE ENFORCER (AUTHORITARIAN PARENT)

"Sleepovers are a bad idea. You need your rest so you don't get sick. Besides, Jane is a little too interested in boys— she'll probably invite some of them, too, and you know you aren't allowed to date. I think you should stay home. We can rent a movie and watch it together."

RESULT: Your concern for your daughter's physical health does not take into account her emotional health. She needs to be with friends and to have fun. You also assume that Jane will make bad choices and imply that your daughter will go along with these bad choices. This is insulting and does not provide an opportunity for your daughter to show you her good judgment. (By the way, your suggestion that she spend a night with the family may seem more like punishment than a fun thing to do.)

THE FRIEND (PERMISSIVE PARENT)

"I like Jane. Sure you can stay with her. I'll pick you up Saturday at noon."

RESULT: Because you ask so few questions, your teenager doesn't give you any details. You don't know if there will be boys or alcohol at the get-together or whether a parent will supervise the party. You trust your teen to make choices for herself that she may not have the good judgment to make.

THE EFFECTIVE PARENT (AUTHORITATIVE PARENT)

"Tell me more about the plans for the evening. Will Jane's parents be home and supervising? Who else is invited? What do you plan to do? Will there be any boys there? You know the rules about no drinking. Can you assure me you'll follow them? It sounds like a fun 'girls' night in.' Sure, you may go—and call me if anything changes."

RESULT: You are making it clear that you have certain expectations about the sleepover, while allowing your daughter to demonstrate that she has thought of all these things too. You are setting limits on her freedom, while still allowing her to have fun, provided she respects the boundaries.

As these exchanges between teens and parents show, it is not always easy to find the right balance between being sensitive to teens' needs and ensuring they remain safe. Whatever our responses, we want to keep the lines of communication open, so we must be respectful of their wishes and needs. At the same time, we must remember that teens want to test limits and experiment and that they don't always have the best judgment about what is safe. We must help them make good decisions by setting fair and reasonable boundaries and expectations, which gradually ease off as they demonstrate responsible behaviour.

WHAT IS AN AUTHORITATIVE PARENTING STYLE?

Authoritative parenting is considered by most experts to be the most effective style of parenting. It consists of striking a balance between sensitivity and firmness, and it is effective for teens as well as younger children. An authoritative parenting style involves balancing sensitivity to your teen's concerns and point of view (that is, paying attention, listening and validating) with the right amount of firmness (that is, offering guidance, maintaining control over choices as appropriate and making your expectations clear). As the term implies, an authoritative parent is knowledgable, reliable and influential, without being overly harsh, critical or too easygoing.

Effective parenting, of course, means more than just balancing sensitivity and firmness. Effective parents clarify issues, give reasons for the limits they may impose, and seek out opportunities for their teen to practise making appropriate and safe decisions. It doesn't mean you have to justify your behaviour or engage in debate; nor does it mean there is no room for discussion: effective parenting requires a respectful dialogue between both parties. If a discussion becomes too heated, the parent relies on his authority to terminate further discussion until emotions are in check.

Adolescents benefit from having parents who express concern and interest (for example, about relevant issues, choices and privileges) while maintaining firmness when it is warranted. Basically, our goal is to make teens feel accepted and in control of their own lives—within reason—so that their views and individuality can develop freely (something we refer to as *autonomy*). However, we need to balance this freedom with clear messages about personal safety and responsibilities. Interestingly, effective teachers, school principals, coaches, work supervisors and even organizations use a similar combination of sensitivity and firmness.

Because an authoritative parenting style is so important to the rest of the strategies outlined in this booklet, take a look at the diagram on the following page entitled Balance in Relationships, so that you fully understand what this concept entails.

WHY AUTHORITATIVE PARENTING MAKES A DIFFERENCE

There is clear evidence that this balance of sensitivity and firmness is beneficial to adolescent development. Firmness acts as a deterrent against problem behaviours, such as alcohol and other drug use, and delinquency. Showing warmth and sensitivity, while making reasonable allowances so that a teen can develop a sense of autonomy, serves to reduce a teen's level of distress and provide an atmosphere of concern and stability.

In contrast, authoritarian parents may see their adolescent's increasing independence as a sign of rebelliousness or disrespect, and they may resist his growing need for autonomy. Unfortunately, teens raised in homes where rules are rigidly enforced and seldom explained tend to have greater difficulty making

Figure 1
BALANCE IN RELATIONSHIPS

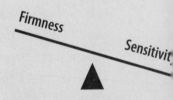

BALANCED

Firmness   Sensitivity

TOO PERMISSIVE

Firmness   Sensitivit

This is the most effective style.

- You have found a balance between listening to your teen's point of view and being firm about what you expect.
- You know your teenager, and you know what limits you must set to keep him safe.
- You know that you will not always be there when a decision has to be made, so you protect your teen by making sure that your expectations are known before they are needed.
- You have managed to balance respect for your teen's needs with your good judgment about boundaries that must be set.

This style (heavy on sensitivity, light on firmness) is too permissive and/or indulgent.

- You are too concerned about your teen's point of view and not enough about setting limits.
- You are too giving, and this means that your teen will take risks because she thinks that you won't care or won't know what's going on.

REMEMBER: The best protection our teens can have against unsafe decisions is to have a clear understanding of what we expect of them. If we've listened to them, they will listen to us. They also have to know the consequences the transition to adolescence. They tend to be either dependent and passive or rebellious and easily influenced by peers as well as being less self-assured and self-guided. These teens often seem more concerned with getting caught and punished for misbehaving than with the principles of right and wrong.

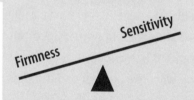

TOO AUTHORITARIAN

Sensitivity

Firmness

- You may be easily fooled into thinking your teen is mature and trustworthy.
- Being too permissive can become too neglectful. You are not involved enough in showing good choices and an adult point of view.

This style (heavy on firmness, light on sensitivity) is too demanding and one sided.
- You are not paying enough attention to your teen's needs or point of view.
- You may think you can dictate what should be done in all situations.
- Your approach is to forbid activities, setting up rules and punishments for mistakes.

- You are not helping your teen to make good choices on his own.
- Your teen will learn to hide things from you and will listen to peers for advice, resulting in riskier behaviours.
- Conflict can escalate and even turn nasty.

of their actions, so that risky behaviour is less attractive than safe behaviour. Working together is the best plan for both parents and teenagers.

When excessive parental control is accompanied by extreme coldness and punishment, a teen may rebel and act out in an attempt to assert his independence and spite his parents. The expression "he's out of control" often means the teen, often out of frustration, has decided to send a message that he has given up on rules altogether—a very dangerous and self-destructive path (of course, parents can go "out of control" too). Remember, your teen doesn't want this to happen just as much as you don't, even if it sometimes doesn't feel that way.

Parenting that is too permissive or indifferent is also linked to negative effects on teens' mental health and development, and can lead to behaviour problems. Adolescents reared in indifferent homes are often impulsive and more likely to be involved in delinquent behaviour. They tend to see themselves as the "leader" in experimenting with sex, alcohol and other drugs. The negative

© ZITS Partnership. Reprinted with special permission of King Feature Syndicate

consequences of such things are less important to them than the attention they receive from peers. Adolescents raised in indulgent, overly permissive households are often less mature, more irresponsible, more conforming to their peers, and less able to take a leadership role.

Why is authoritative parenting the best strategy? Authoritative parenting provides an *emotional context* to the everyday discussions that parents and teens have and to the decisions they make. It may be helpful to remember these three things:

- Showing interest and involvement in a teen's life makes him more receptive to parental influence and, by extension, more likely to follow rules. This involves spending time with your teen.
- Talk about your views on various things—parties, alcohol, drugs, schoolwork, jobs—and listen to your teen's—don't just shut down or simply grant permission whenever they ask for it. Such discussion helps teens develop the ability to think for themselves and make better choices.
- By showing sensitivity and offering support, authoritative parents encourage their teen to develop her own self-control, which is a requirement for becoming a responsible, competent individual.

Place an emphasis on safety, responsibility and obeying rules

Let's begin with a simple reminder. When your child was growing up, one of your highest priorities was keeping her safe. Each morning you reminded her of the rules: You made her fasten her seatbelt, wear a helmet, hold an adult's hand when crossing the street and you reminded her not to speak to strangers; later on, you made her keep you informed about where she was going and who she was with. Your child's safety was a priority—something you never questioned and always kept in the forefront—and safety was a requirement in each new situation or decision made.

You made decisions about safety for your child and watched to make sure he listened because you knew he had lessons to learn. Similarly, he expected you to be concerned about his safety, and he seldom questioned your motivation—after all, why would he want to do something that might get him hurt or in trouble?

Now she's an adolescent. Safety is still a critical priority, but your daughter often relies on her own judgment to determine if a situation is safe. Her judgment is also influenced by her friends and other factors, such as her values and even the vast world of telecommunications, media and entertainment that she's in touch with every day. (According to studies, teens spend six hours and 32 minutes each day viewing television and commercial or self-recorded videos as well as movies. They are also exposed to other media and forms of entertainment, including video games, print, radio, recorded music, cellphones, computers and the Internet!)

You can't ensure that you can keep your son safe (and you still worry as you did when he was small), but you can still do your best to help your teen keep himself as safe as possible. The principle remains the same as before: You are his parent, and it's your job to help him make safe and reasonable decisions. If you communicate this message in a purposeful and loving way, you are more likely to be listened to. Here's an example:

[handwritten notes]

Set Rules - / Boundaries — Child -

Safety

Responsible.

Independ.

Fitting in

ANOTHER COMMON DIALOGUE BETWEEN PARENTS AND TEENS

Teen: *"A guy at school asked me to go to a movie with him on Friday night. May I go?"*

THE ENFORCER (AUTHORITARIAN PARENT)

"You know better than to ask me that! The rule is absolutely no dating before your 16th birthday. You are much too young to be going out with a boy. No, you may not go."

RESULT: Clearly you do not understand your daughter's need to develop relationships with boys. Your concern about her dating at a young age is valid, but perhaps this activity could include a group of friends in a harmless social gathering. Consider other ways to keep your teen safe, rather than just forbidding her to take part in activities. How will she learn to make good choices if she is never allowed to make any choices?

THE FRIEND (PERMISSIVE PARENT)

"What's he like? This is your first date! How exciting. I can help you with your hair and makeup if you want."

RESULT: You need to know more about the prospective date. Is the boy your daughter's age or older? What movie is he planning to take her to see? How will they get there and back? You need to make sure that she is safe before you let her go. Remember: the earlier risky behaviours begin, the more serious the possible negative consequences become.

THE EFFECTIVE PARENT (AUTHORITATIVE PARENT)

"Tell me about this boy. What's he like? How do you know him? Would it be just the two of you, or are others going? What movie are you thinking of seeing? I'm not really comfortable with your dating yet. Can we come up with a solution that makes both you and us happy? What if we drive you and your friend to and from the movie theatre? That way we'll at least get to meet him, and we'll be sure you get home when you're supposed to."

RESULT: You are justifiably cautious about letting your daughter go on a date with someone you have not met, but you are keeping the lines of communication open by asking questions. If others are going, the activity is a normal one for young teens to experience. If no one else is invited, an exclusive relationship should be discouraged at too young an age. ("Too young" is up to you, but before age 15 is a reasonable guide.) Your willingness to compromise will help keep your daughter safe. If she chooses not to compromise, you explain that she will not be allowed to go, as your job is to set reasonable boundaries for her.

As shown in the previous example, you may not want your daughter to go out with someone you've never met because you feel it's not safe or appropriate at her age, unless certain rules are established first. In other situations, you might similarly question what your son does after school, because it might not be safe or appropriate. You tell him the rules (such as no drinking, no drugs, no riding in cars with people who have been drinking, curfew at 11 p.m.) not because of arbitrary age-related or legal restrictions, but because you want him to be safe and responsible, and to be trusted to follow the rules.

Because your teen is still developing his own ability to judge risks and rewards, it's often necessary for us to make decisions in the interest of safety or other factors. Your priorities—safety, responsibility and following the rules—may trump your teen's priorities of independence, fitting in and having a good time. Striking the right balance between sensitivity and firmness, straight from the beginning, sets the tone for future discussion and joint decision making.

WHAT YOU DO—AND HOW YOU DO IT—MATTERS!

Whether you like it or not, your teen (like most others) will eventually try alcohol and some other drugs, have sex, and meet new and different people (not all of whom you may approve of). Even if he doesn't do these things, rest assured that his friends are putting pressure on him to do so. Rather than trying to control these rapid changes by force or other means, the central issue for you is to offer guidance and to maintain consistency and safety. By emphasizing safety, rather than simply dictating rules and the consequences of disobeying them, you will maintain the same familiar and important role you have had from the beginning.

Your teen will respect this familiar yet changing role—even if he argues about it at times—because you are both doing your job. His job is to establish his own identity and independence (sometimes at a pace that may seem alarming), and your job is to encourage his personal growth while also emphasizing the importance of making safer choices and delaying decisions that carry risks.

Even if your child has not begun to engage in any of the behaviours mentioned here, she may be pressured to do so or may be faced with situations in which her friends are putting themselves at risk. It's not easy—for her or for you. Fitting in with peers is critical for teens, and parents often feel shut out of their children's lives. Nonetheless, providing your teen with proper warnings and advice will still influence her choices, even if it doesn't seem to do so at the time. Studies repeatedly show that parents continue to have an enormous influence on their children's behaviour during adolescence. So make no mistake: *You do make a difference.*

To remain important in your teen's life and to be most effective, though, you have to be sensitive to how your teen is changing and how your role may change. Fathers and mothers who take an appropriate interest in their teen's activities and whereabouts, and who provide appropriate rules and restrictions in the context of a positive, engaging overall relationship, help their teen develop a more firmly grounded and positive view of himself in relation to others.

Thus it is not just what we do in response to situations with our teen that matters; the emotional context in which we do it also matters. Teens have very sensitive emotional antennae and are adept at reading their parents' moods and body language, and at timing their requests. Sometimes they're on more familiar ground if they get emotionally charged up and expect us to react the same way.

You can avoid this emotional trap if you set the tone: Remember to stick to the issue at hand and to communicate your view or decision in an atmosphere of support.

3 Wods
* Body Language - Strongest Weight
2 Voice Tone.

Sin

Teach—don't just criticize

Adolescence often tops parents' list of concerns when they are asked what aspect of their child's development they are most worried about . But much of this worry stems from widespread and distorted stereotypes that adolescents are difficult, moody and bad-tempered.

Contrary to popular belief, only a small proportion of families (between five and 10 per cent) experience a dramatic deterioration in the quality of the parent-child relationship during adolescence. Rather than treating your teen in a way that is overly cautious or harsh, your goal should be to encourage him to gradually become mature, responsible and independent. If you succeed in doing this, you will have made the most of this important time.

However, if, instead, we adhere to outdated myths and stereotypes about teenagers, you may leave your teen with the impression that she is making your life miserable. Let's examine a few of the most common myths about teens so that we can start with a fresh perspective:

MYTH 1: "THE TEEN YEARS ARE THE WORST!"

Teens are expected to be troublesome and aggravate their parents, right? Wrong. As researchers began to challenge stereotyped views of adolescence, they discovered that three out of four teens (75 per cent) reported happy and pleasant relation-ships with their parents—and that the remaining 25 per cent of teens who were not so happy had histories of difficulties that preceded adolescence. The classic generation gap that has been widely promoted and popularized in our culture as the explanation for parents' problems with teens has been dealt a critical blow. Most teens want to spend time with their parents.

Yet, despite this fact, most books about adolescence still emphasize conflict, implicitly blaming adolescence itself for the trouble parents experience. For the most part, the perception remains that adolescence is a difficult time and that teens are puzzling, troublesome, angry and ungrateful.

This overblown stereotype can affect how we react to the normal things teens do. So be careful not to jump to conclusions that might be self-fulfilling! You can expect a fair amount of stress and conflict as your teen develops, but try to enjoy this time of transition. Keep in mind that, in all likelihood, a few years from now you will have a strong and rewarding adult relationship, and the daily hassles will be long forgotten.

MYTH 2: "EVERYTHING TURNS INTO AN ARGUMENT!"

Parents say this often, and it usually reflects the frustration they experience as they try to resolve daily hassles with their teen. But you might be surprised to know that a bit of stress can be a good thing. Experts believe that the many daily hassles we experience in raising a teen, typically those related to issues of independence, serve as "dry runs" for the teen's efforts to establish herself as an independent adult. Although it might seem hard to accept at first, arguments and disagreements are normal, and they may even prove helpful!

Anyone who lives with a teenager knows that a certain amount of conflict is inevitable. In fact, researchers suggest that teens have an average of seven disagreements per day! Moms take the brunt of it, followed by siblings, then friends and finally romantic partners. In typical families, fathers, other peers and adults are much further down the list. The most common conflicts concern curfews, choice of friends and activities, chores, alcohol and other substance use, school work, discipline, household rules, involvement in illicit activities and communication difficulties.

But these conflicts are a normal part of growing up. Most are not angry, intense battles (although some may be), but more like role plays that help teens develop communication and conflict-resolution skills. Teenagers must learn how to resolve conflicts in their lives, and parents, siblings and peers assist them with this task (willingly or not). Think of these situations as a training ground where teens can develop the skills to resolve bigger issues later on.

MYTH 3: "I CAN'T REASON WITH HER—SHE DOESN'T LISTEN!"

frontal cortex not all develp. til 25.

Adolescence is certainly not conflict-free. However, the way we as parents experience conflicts may differ from our teen's experience of them. Mothers, fathers and teenagers actually experience interactions with one another in very different ways. Experts believe that parents are more bothered by bickering than teens are. As psychologist Lawrence Steinberg explains in his 1997 book, *You and Your*

Adolescent (see Resources), the reason for this is linked to the nature of adolescent development: You may experience and describe arguments differently than your teen does because parents typically frame the issue in terms of right and wrong. But for teens, the same issue is often seen as a matter of personal choice.

To illustrate this important difference in how parents and teens view the same issue, Steinberg uses the example of maintaining a clean room. Parents usually feel this is important because it's the "right thing to do," whereas teens see the state of their room as their own business (a little bit of personal autonomy, you might say).

This difference in perception may also help to explain why parents and teens feel differently after a conflict. Parents often see conflict as a (bad) reflection of how they are raising their child, so they conclude that their son or daughter is intentionally rejecting their values, which may seem like a deliberate violation of their expectations. (A voice in their head may shout, "In my day my mom would knock some sense into me!")

Teens, however, attach far less meaning to such conflict. In their view, there's nothing particularly rebellious or nasty about it. It's just time for them to show some autonomy. (They may say, "It's my room. Why should you care?") For this reason it's usually the parent, not the adolescent, who gets upset and who continues to feel that way for some time.

Pick Your Battles.

MYTH 4: "MY TEEN PUSHES MY BUTTONS" (THIS MAY BE PARTLY TRUE…)

Although parent-child conflict in adolescence is normal, it can still take a toll, especially on parents! The transitions your child is going through are indeed stressful—for him as well as for you—and they can have a significant effect on your mental health and other relationships. Even though upsetting conflicts over day-to-day issues seldom destroy the parent-child relationship, their repetitive nature can take a toll on parents' mental health and well-being.

Mothers of daughters and fathers of sons show more psychological distress, report less satisfaction with their marriage, and experience more doubt and worry as their children begin to mature physically, get involved in dating relationships and distance themselves from their parents emotionally. Parents who have strong connections with friends, colleagues and with each other may be buffered from some of these negative consequences, whereas single parents may be especially vulnerable to them.

© ZITS Partnership. Reprinted with special permission of King Feature Syndicate

Parents who are emotionally distressed (for example, they may feel depressed, anxious or self-doubting) feel less effective and are less effective as parents. If you feel this way, try to focus on your role and what you are trying to accomplish, and try not to worry.

Thinking of our parenting role as one of teaching, rather than demanding, is a more realistic way to approach this complex task. As teachers, our job is to point out what we know about things we want our teen to learn, including the good with the not so good. Teens often look for the "yes, but" side of an argument. So if we only lecture them about the downside of things (for example, warning them about the dangers of alcohol and other drugs), they will naturally be curious about the upside (for example, they may ask, "Then why do you like to drink?"). An effective teacher—and parent—teaches students how to think for themselves and become more self-reliant. Teens are savvy, so it pays to teach them to weigh the risks and benefits of engaging in new and enticing activities, while avoiding absolutes that they can too easily reject.

Listen to them –
Empathy.
Brain storm w/ them Have them
come up w/ problems solves.

Understand your teen's development— and how it affects your relationship

The question is not whether your relationship with your child will change during adolescence, but rather in what way, to what degree and with what effect. Studies show it's common for adolescents to perceive their relationship with their parents in a less positive light than they did as young children: by age 14, most teens report more parent-child conflicts and less parental involvement in their lives. They also report feeling less positively about their parents (and vice versa). This is normal.

More than any other stage of development, adolescence seems like an endless series of crises. These crises, of course, are an extension of familiar adaptive processes that offer opportunities for growth, much like the first day of school or the first night away from home.

Teens face considerable stress and new challenges. They need to be seen as unique, all the while fitting in with others and what others expect. Of special concern for some teenagers are the added issues of cultural identity and sexual orientation, which are critical if those things make them different from the majority. The demands of culture and the demands of society may pull teens in different directions, placing even more pressure on them to make difficult choices.

[handwritten margin notes: child needs to feel love, capable, self-esteem, make decisions, give BK to the world]

ASSERTING INDEPENDENCE

To understand who they are and where they are heading in life, teenagers must feel a sense of independence and achievement. They want to be seen as self-sufficient and therefore must become less emotionally dependent on their parents. Teens strive to assert their independence: they need to start making their own decisions and to establish a personal set of values and morals.

At the same time, they still need to be connected to their families, since families provide the safety platform from which all new ventures are launched. The family also can be a place of refuge when experiments go wrong. But teenagers' attempts to balance their freedom with a sense of connectedness to family can lead to "push-pull" behaviour. Teens can be affectionate with parents one moment and aloof the next. They can be the child you've known for years or an unexpected stranger. These dramatic variations all form part of their efforts to establish a separate identity from their parents and siblings and from the identity they had as a child. They may say to you, for example, "I'm not a kid anymore."

PHYSICAL AND EMOTIONAL CHANGES

You might be surprised to know that adolescence involves more biological, psychological and social role changes than any other stage of life except infancy. This period offers tremendous opportunity for establishing the skills and values needed for adult life. At the same time, however, it is associated with greater risk than any other period in terms of academic failure, violence and health-compromising behaviours.

Consider that your 12-year-old child has probably established comfortable and important relationships with you, her siblings and other adults, and is eager to find her own identity. A mere seven years later, she will be on the verge of assuming adult responsibilities and will be expected to become fully independent. Is it any wonder, then, that parents need assistance in understanding how to be of greatest benefit to their teen.

Let's look at some of the major changes that occur during adolescence.

APPEARANCE AND BEHAVIOUR

Physical changes are the most visible changes and can affect how teens view themselves and how they interact with others. Just as teens are becoming more self-aware, they must deal with rapid growth spurts and hormonal changes that may increase their feelings of insecurity or self-consciousness. Being among the first or the last students in a class to deal with these changes only complicates this process.

Of course, there are also marked changes during adolescence in the way teens behave, as their ways of thinking and perceiving others evolve. One central change occurs in the context of relationships, as teens begin to shift the balance of influence from the family to peers. As they strive to develop an identity, they attempt to draw apart from family members and to form more intense relationships with peers. From the ages of 12 to 15, there is usually a gradual move away from involvement with groups of the same sex to mixed groups, and eventually toward romantic partnerships.

BRAIN DEVELOPMENT AND JUDGMENT

There are also important changes taking place in the adolescent brain that parents should know about. The part of the brain where emotional control, impulse restraint and rational decision making take place grows quickly during the teenage years. However, because this part of the brain is still developing, many teens cannot always exercise self-control, and they can misjudge the possible consequences of their actions.

As they develop, teenagers' intellectual capabilities become more sophisticated, their expectations about relationships become more realistic, and their abilities to control their emotions become more finely tuned. Their reasoning and problem-solving abilities improve over time, and this means that their more advanced thinking skills make it possible for them to see a situation from more than one point of view. They can take into account what *might* happen as well as what is happening, and they can use this information to think about themselves, relationships and the world in a more complete manner.

Immature brain development helps to explain why experimenting with alcohol, other drugs and sex can be particularly risky. Teens' curiosity and interest are piqued, but they lack the judgment and knowledge needed to delay gratification and make safer choices. And there is recent evidence that some substances, especially alcohol, can have a long-term harmful effect on brain development, specifically in terms of memory. Teens need to understand that binge drinking, in particular, can cause permanent damage because it interferes with ongoing brain development.

SELF-AWARENESS

As teens mature, they can plan ahead, anticipate the responses of others and debate and argue more effectively. On the upside, this increased understanding of their own emotions and the ability to analyze why they feel a certain way makes it possible for them to have more intimate relationships with others. On the downside, they may become too self-absorbed or feel that everyone else is watching and judging them. Choices concerning their relationships, interests and well-being also originate in adolescence, and these can last a lifetime.

At this point in their lives, teenagers begin to shift their focus and interests from their families to their peers and separate their "family self" from their "peer self." They will want more privacy from family members, and they will look to friends for answers to questions. While parents need to gradually let go of their dominant role, they still need to maintain an active presence. Peers may provide excellent advice about superficial decisions such as what clothes to wear, but parents still have influence in important matters such as moral values, safety, school performance, finances and future goals.

Understand the pressures—
and the risks—your teen faces

PRESSURES TO DRINK, SMOKE AND HAVE SEX

Here is a really scary fact for parents: Between the ages of 11 and 16, most adolescents begin to experiment in various ways with cigarettes, alcohol, other drugs and sex. They do so partly because of pressure from peers, but also because these activities form part of the rite of passage into adulthood. Whether you like it or not, they will be exposed to many temptations—and they will need guidance (not threats) to get through this stage.

We would all like to think that our children can resist these pressures and make smart choices, but common sense and statistics tell us that they need help. Every teenager will have to make choices about whether or not to get involved in these risky behaviours. Some will be influenced by their peers to experiment. Others will become bystanders, choosing to watch but not take part. Some may act as "crisis counsellors," encouraging their friends to make safer choices and offering them support if things go wrong.

As part of our research with adolescents, we asked more than 1,400 teens from 10 schools in Southwestern Ontario some questions about their use of alcohol and other drugs, their involvement in sexual activity, and their experiences of

Figure 2
TEENS BINGE DRINKING

**Steady Increase in Binge Drinking
from Grade 7 to 10**

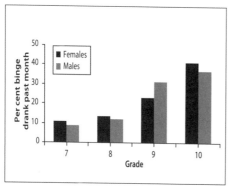

Figure 3
TEENS USING MARIJUANA

**Steady Increase in Marijuana Use
from Grade 7 to 10**

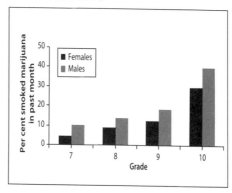

Figure 4
TEENS SEXUALLY ACTIVE

**Sharp Rise in Sexual Activity
from Grade 7 to 10**

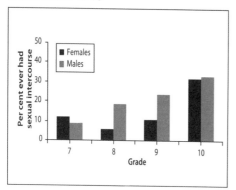

Figure 5
DATING VIOLENCE

**Sharp Increase in Dating Violence
from Grade 9 to 10**

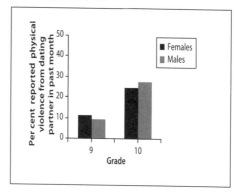

being hit by a dating partner. In Figures 2–5 you'll see the clear pattern that emerges across these risk behaviours: there is a steady increase in binge drinking, marijuana use, sexual intercourse and dating violence from grades 7 to 10.

By Grade 10, about 40 per cent of girls and boys report binge drinking over the past month (defined as having five or more drinks on one occasion); 30 per cent of girls and 40 per cent of boys have recently smoked marijuana; 25 per cent have had sexual intercourse; and about 30 per cent have experienced physical violence from a dating partner in the past month.

These figures are in line with other studies conducted across North America, and they point to the fact that experimentation with substance use and sex, and being treated abusively by a dating partner, are, unfortunately, common occurrences.

PRESSURES TO BE SEEN AS TOUGH (BOYS) OR POPULAR (GIRLS)

When your child was very young, he or she quickly learned the differences between men and women, boys and girls. Splitting the world into simpler categories actually helps young children learn more quickly, which is a good thing. This simplified but very biased view of the world around them eases off during middle childhood as they begin to feel more comfortable relating not only to children of their own sex but to those of the opposite sex as well.

However, by early adolescence, there are once again enormous pressures and new things to figure out. For most boys and girls, this pressure translates into a need to be accepted and fit in, which means the need to look, act and dress the way their peers do. Although most teens won't admit it, they are compelled to display outward signs (for example, the right shoes, hairstyle, jeans and music) that send a clear message that they are a boy or a girl and that they "get it."

Boys, for example, are pressured to be tough and are rewarded for excelling in traditional male pursuits (for example, athletics and leadership roles). The male "jock" is still the most popular and respected person on most high school campuses. Girls, on the other hand, are rewarded for being nice, and their popularity rises when they succeed at traditional female pursuits (for example, attractive appearance and having many male and female friends).

Because of strong cultural expectations and biases, such expressions of boy-ness or girl-ness are fairly normal. However, one of the many pitfalls of this rigid gender pressure on teens is that it forces some to give up things that they were once good at, because these things might not be considered okay anymore. For example, athletic abilities become highly sought after in boys so, by implication, they diminish in importance for girls. In fact, between ages 12 and 15, girls drop out of athletic activities at an alarming rate, regardless of their previous abilities.

Likewise, attributes that are viewed as attractive in girls, such as intimacy and emotional expression, are avoided by boys if they want to be accepted by their male peers, who are on the lookout for any signs of "gayness" (see the section following, entitled "Pressures to put others down"). Boys who may have an interest in music or art, for example, may be pressured to prove their masculinity by behaving aggressively or in a hyper-masculine way in other activities. Similarly, girls who have an interest in sports may try to exaggerate their femininity in other areas to avoid possible ridicule by peers.

At the other extreme, some boys and girls choose instead to totally reject the popular route and form their own clusters of like-minded individuals, usually distinguishable by their unique style of hair, clothes and music. Although belonging to a subculture provides a sense of identity and common interests, students still experience the abusive pressures that are embedded in the majority culture of the school.

Teen boys come to believe that in order to fit in with what their peers expect they need to be very different from girls in as many ways as possible and, to a lesser extent, the same holds true for girls, who feel the need to be different from boys. For boys, sticking to the most visible and desirable male characteristics is the safest route to peer acceptance—and avoiding being verbally or physically attacked.

PRESSURES TO FIT IN

As a parent, you probably know that one of the strongest—yet often unnoticed —pressures for teens is the pressure to conform to what other teens decide is acceptable. This is why the majority of teens strive to wear the right clothes, listen to the right music and participate in the right activities both in and out of school. Such vigilance, of course, is pretty normal and part of growing up. Teens are experts at recognizing what is "cool" or "uncool," and they patrol one another to ensure that they don't cross the line.

Although we all faced them, these pressures are not harmless. Each day they go to school, many teens worry about being humiliated, teased, threatened or hurt—sometimes by the same "friends" they hung out with a few days ago. Something goes wrong—she wore the wrong shoes, said the wrong thing or dated the wrong guy—and her world changes almost overnight. To manage these pressures to be seen by others as nice or tough, teens sometimes feel they have to display their loyalties, even if it means hurting others.

Conforming to the culture of the school is not easy, and it sometimes leads to feelings of frustration, anger, rebelliousness or depression and hopelessness. Such responses are especially acute for those who seek more individuality, who have non-traditional interests, who come from different countries or cultural backgrounds, who have a different sexual orientation, or who are different in any noticeable way from the mainstream. These teens account for a sizeable minority of every school, yet they face the greater risk of being teased, bullied or harassed by members of their own sex and by the opposite sex.

PRESSURES TO PUT OTHERS DOWN

Being called "gay" is the most common insult in our schools today, surpassing racist and sexist insults that have become more strictly forbidden. Because adults (this includes all of us: parents, educators, clergy and all others who influence youth in our communities) have not spoken out against homophobic insults, they have become implicitly accepted and commonplace. Being gay is so stigmatized in our society that one of the worst insults is to call someone gay, whether they are or not. Such insults are a visible demonstration of how teens patrol their borders to ensure conformity to gender and similar expectations. As parents, we need to let teens know that hurling insults at someone or having to hide who they are is unacceptable.

Homophobic insults and abusive language that stigmatizes those who seem different ("That's so gay!" and "He's too weird!") explode during early- to mid-adolescence, and this pattern shows signs of worsening. In fact, the biggest change in the type of harassment experienced by teens over the last decade is the incidence of being called gay or lesbian. Boys, in particular, find it necessary to police their own and others' behaviours to defend themselves against humiliation and not being considered adequately masculine. Like racist and sexist insults, homophobic insults stem from ignorance and create an atmosphere of suspicion, fear and intolerance.

Vilifying others as "gay" or "weird" serves the misguided function of elevating teens' status with peers by demonstrating that they have "the right stuff." Not surprisingly, boys see homophobic insults as insignificant (they claim to be "just joking"), much as they do negative comments about girls and women. Of course, such attitudes and pressures also justify boys' (and sometimes girls') abusive language and acts toward others, especially those who do not fit masculine stereotypes.

PRESSURES TO DO WELL AT SCHOOL

Homework assignments and worry about marks are perhaps the most common forms of stress during adolescence. As the workload increases during the high school years, more and more students feel they have too much work and worry about keeping up. On top of the increasing and more challenging workload, teens also report feeling a greater degree of pressure to achieve—from teachers, parents and even their peers. Interestingly, boys report feeling more pressure in Grade 6, and girls in Grade 10.

Significantly, students' academic performance and successes are positively linked to parental *support*, but negatively linked to parental pressure to achieve high marks. In fact, instead of motivating teens, such pressure can have the opposite effect, leading some teens to disengage from academic activities.

The importance of feeling connected to school, without undue pressure, was highlighted in a survey of more than 7000 Canadian youth (ages 10 to 16).[1] How students felt about themselves overall was strongly related to how they felt about their lives at school. In fact, students who felt less pressure from parents to achieve high marks reported the highest perceived achievement and school satisfaction! These students viewed their relationships with their teachers and their parents in more positive ways and had higher self-esteem than students who felt pressured to obtain high marks.

THE RELATIONSHIP CONNECTION

Figure 6 points out one thing that isn't always obvious: risky behaviours, such as substance use, peer and dating violence, and precocious sexual behaviour, take place in the context of relationships. Teens attempt these activities because they

---

[1] Boyce, W. (Ed.). (2003). *The Health Behaviour of School Age Children: The Canadian Report*. Ottawa, Ontario: Health Canada. For more information about the HBSC study, please visit www.hbsc.org.

Figure 6
CIRCULARITY OF RISK BEHAVIOURS

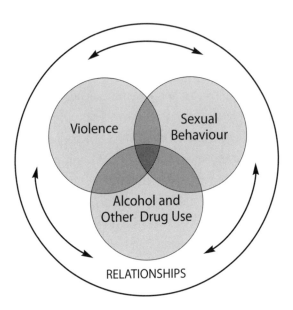

want to fit in, feel more grown up and try out things that they couldn't try before. Relationships can add to the pressures and risks, but they also can protect.

This relationship context reflects developmental circumstances, such as resolving disputes with parents or peers, seeking status or acceptance, or seeking new pleasures. Thus, it often comes down to the individual's skill at negotiating relationship issues, particularly with parents, peers and romantic partners, which determines his or her degree of risk.

In addition to the relationship context, some activities partially overlap; for example, teens who report binge drinking also report marijuana use, sexual activity and dating violence. We sometimes refer to this as the triad of risk behaviours (*see Figure 6*), because they are linked by common causes, situations and desires. It also reminds us that if a teen is known to be experimenting with one of these activities, he is likely to be trying the others as well. For example, studies tell us that alcohol use is a common denominator in other unsafe activities, such as smoking, sexual activity, drinking and driving, and abuse.

"WHAT MESSAGE DO I GIVE?"

As parents, we need to recognize that some experimentation is normal and that it can even have a purpose. Whether you like it or not, simply forbidding or punishing such behaviour may drive teens further away. Our message should be one of concern, with clear communication about personal safety, choice and

© ZITS Partnership. Reprinted with special permission of King Feature Syndicate

responsibility. However, our message of concern should also point out the consequences of overstepping whatever limits we have set.

Similarly, we are responsible for helping our children succeed by motivating them and offering encouragement. However, we must also have realistic expectations and avoid adding to the pressure in our teens' lives.

So where does this leave us? Because adolescence is a time when individuals prepare to take on adult roles and privileges, some amount of experimentation and transition is necessary. The issue becomes when, how and with what adolescents will experiment, as well as what role adults should play in ensuring teens make safe and responsible choices. As parents, we must accept the reality of these behaviour patterns and strike an appropriate balance between sensitivity and firmness.

The simple message is that parents need to do all they can to offer their teen encouragement and support and to show genuine interest in her social and academic life. While it is important to supervise your teen's homework and her academic performance, make sure your expectations are realistic and not coupled with guilt or fear. One 15-year-old explained it this way to parents: "Doing well is something that I have to do for myself, but I could use your support."

Practical strategies to promote safer choices and healthy relationships: 10 tips for parents

Over the past 50 years or so we've learned quite a bit about what influences teens' poor choices, as well as what keeps them safer. Some of the negative influences lie at the level of the individual teen. For example, rebelliousness, favourable attitudes to antisocial behaviour (including drug use and violence), and beliefs that certain risks are outweighed by the benefits are common descriptors of teens who end up in trouble.

Other negative influences occur at the peer level. For example, socializing with troublemakers, having friends who use alcohol and other drugs, and getting recognition and acceptance from others for taking risks or being violent are the most common findings in studies of teens with problems.

Finally, negative influences on teen risk behaviours can occur at the level of the family, school, and even the broader community and culture. Some of the strongest predictors of negative teen outcomes are: inadequate schools, having fewer opportunities for success, having family members who abuse substances or are violent, and poor parenting methods. Likewise, teens who grow up in unsafe neighbourhoods, where they are exposed to crime and where alcohol and other drugs can be easily obtained increase the likelihood that a teen will have trouble remaining safe.

On the other hand, youths who have assets such as positive life experiences and certain personal qualities, such as common sense and compassion, are likely to become healthy, caring and responsible adults. Youth assets also include things like success or accomplishment in schoolwork, sports, peer groups and volunteer activities. Creativity and musical ability are additional assets. Assets can be internal (such as academic or musical ability) or external (such as involvement in voluntary services and peer committees). Healthy relationships with family members, peers and other important adults help build teens' self-esteem and confidence. During the critical adolescent years, assets have the power to influence the choices young people make and to help them become successful and responsible adults.

The extent to which teens can call on their many assets has a strong influence on the number of positive choices they will make as they mature. Research has shown that the greater the number of assets young people have, the more positive and successful their development will be. Conversely, the fewer assets they have, the greater the possibility they will engage in risky behaviours, such as drug use, unsafe sex and violence.

Assets powerfully influence youths' behaviour by protecting them from risky situations and by promoting positive attitudes and choices. This influence reaches across cultural and socio-economic groups of youth and extends from childhood to young adulthood.

So, what's the best type of protection from negative influences? You guessed it: healthy relationships. We know that one of the best factors for reducing risk among teens is having a positive connection with caring adults: parents, other family members, teachers, coaches, faith leaders and other community members provide balance in the lives of teens who are besieged with pressures.

Here are some tips for building and maintaining healthy relationships with your teen:

1. **Be honest and open.**

   Research shows that the more open and honest you are with your teen, the more communication there will be about dating and sexuality, and other topics too. And talking to your teen about dating and sexuality is very important because a good predictor of less adolescent sex is directly related to how much parents and teens openly discuss sex. In-depth discussions about dating and sexuality are one mechanism by which a better quality parent-teen relationship can influence an adolescent's choice to delay sexual activity. Your discussions should reveal your attitudes and values about sexuality and include advice and warnings about potentially negative consequences of teenage sexual activity, including the transmission of disease. For some parents, this may also mean making sure older teens have condoms and birth control.

2. **Be authoritative—not authoritarian or permissive— in your parenting style.**

   Show an authoritative parenting style, which involves a combination of sensitivity and firmness. Set high standards and have high expectations for your teen regarding his behaviour, and enforce these standards with consistent discipline. At the same time, provide an atmosphere of warmth and acceptance where the teen's views and individuality can develop freely.

3. **Think in terms of harm reduction instead of zero tolerance.**

   It is unrealistic to assume that teens will not experiment with adult privileges such as substance use, romance and sex. Parents who try to enforce absolutes often develop conflicts with their teens and most often are not told about their teens' activities. The alternative to this inflexible attitude is to discuss choices and the pros and cons of these new-found opportunities with your teen in a non-threatening manner and to obtain their understanding in advance of what the consequences will be if they break your trust. Convey to them that you want them to be safe, which implies that they must take responsibility for their actions, use their own judgment and make their own choices.

4. **Don't believe everything you read or hear.**

   The media would have us believe that drug use, heavy drinking, violence and underage sex are occurring at rates far greater than they actually are. These misconceptions can lead to a sense of dread as your child approaches the teen years and may influence how you react to your child's behaviour. This is especially true if you automatically assume that she will become involved in high-risk behaviour. Get the facts and examine the misconceptions you may have about your teen's behaviour before you jump to any conclusions.

5. **Monitor and supervise your teen's activities with sensitivity.**

   Parental supervision is a key factor that can moderate adolescent problem behaviour. However, you need to balance monitoring your teen's behaviour with sensitivity so you do not become over-intrusive and unnecessarily invade his privacy. You can monitor your child's activities simply by being present (for example, before and after he goes out) and by asking a few simple questions in a neutral (non-accusatory) tone. Too much supervision and monitoring can lead to greater problem behaviour, because teens may rebel to exercise their right to some freedom from parental constraints.

6. **Accentuate the positive.**
   Try to initiate positive communication with your teenager whenever the opportunity arises. If you are experiencing conflict (for example, over rules, chores, school work or peers), talk to her about it, but also attempt to have positive conversations with your teen about other things. The fact that you have a conflict does not mean that every interaction has to be negative. Actively attempt to build in genuine positive interactions throughout the day or week so that your teen knows that you feel unhappy with her behaviour and not with her as a person.

7. **Encourage your teen to be involved in extracurricular activities.**
   Studies have shown that greater extracurricular involvement at school or in the community can have a positive influence on a teen's academic achievement and on pro-social behaviours such as voting and volunteering in young adulthood. Be aware! Girls drop out of sports and other physical activities at an alarming rate when they get to high school, because they are pressured into believing that being athletic is not feminine. Speak with them about these pressures and why it is important for them to make their own decisions.

8. **Encourage flexibility in gender roles and behaviour.**

   Teens are under considerable pressure to conform to their peers' (and some-times family's) expectations about what boys and girls "should and should not do." Gender-role rigidity is very high in early to mid-adolescence. At this time, boys, in particular, have a heightened sense of the importance of being "mas-culine." Speak to them about these pressures and their views, and encourage them to recognize how some of their choices (for example, choices related to friends and sports) may be misdirected by fears of being ridiculed. Overly aggressive and controlling behaviour in male teens is often a sign of their strict adherence to societal expectations, which parents can inadvertently reinforce by using expressions such as "be a man" or "tough it out"). Discuss ways to respond to teasing in a light-hearted manner.

9. **Address the use of abusive or inappropriate language with a firm and clear message.**

   Today it has become acceptable in teen culture to swear and verbally abuse others like no previous generation has done. While parents can't totally prevent abusive language from coming into their homes (for example, via music, television and other media), teens appreciate knowing the limits. Language is a powerful means by which teens control the actions of others, including dating partners, parents and peers. Be especially vigilant about expressions they use that put down others, no matter how innocent or joking they may seem, and point out what these expressions really communicate.

10. Be an active participant in your teen's life.

Know your teen's interests. If she likes hockey, take her to a hockey game if you can. If she plays hockey, watch her play—in a non-critical way. If your teen likes opera, ballet or has another interest, plan a day when you can be together to do something special. Or if a movie comes on television that you both like, watch it together. Few words need to be spoken. Being together is what counts!

Write an encouragement letter to your child.

Resources for parents

TOP PICKS

These two books are reader friendly and up to date, and they offer good examples of positive parenting and adolescent development:

Steinberg, L. & Levine, A. (1997). *You and Your Adolescent: A Parent's Guide for Ages 10–20* (revised edition). New York: HarperCollins.

Wolf, A. E. (2002). *Get Out of My Life, but first could you drive me and Cheryl to the mall? A Parent's Guide to the New Teenager.* New York: Farrar, Straus & Giroux.

SPECIFIC THEMES

Popular books that contain advice for parents with teenagers widely acknowledge the changing nature of the parent-child relationship during adolescence and discuss its impact on family members. Several themes emerge in current books for parents and teens, focusing on basic problems and solutions.

THE COMBINED EFFECTS OF POP CULTURE AND PEERS

Taffel, R. & Blau, M. (2001). *The Second Family: Dealing with Peer Power, Pop Culture, the Wall of Silence—and Other Challenges of Raising Today's Teens.* New York: St. Martin's Griffin.

Taffel and Blau point to the reality that families of teens are competing with a "second family" composed of peers and pop culture. Parents face the challenge of remaining both aware of, and vigilant about, the positive and negative effects of this powerful influence.

COMMUNICATING WITH TEENS IN THE AGE OF TECHNOLOGY

Grigsby, C. & Julian, K. (2002). *How to Get Your Teen to Talk to You*. Sisters, OR: Multnomah Publishers.

For decades, experts on raising teenagers have emphasized the importance of establishing good communication between parents and their adolescents. This challenge is heightened by the fact that communication between parents and teens may be at an all-time low due to competition from technology and media. Not only are adolescents spending more time in front of computers and televisions, they are also acquiring knowledge at a lightning speed that parents cannot keep up with. Parents need to strike a balance between supporting their teen's need for an independent identity and strengthening the parent-child relationship through non-judgmental communication.

UNDERSTANDING ADOLESCENT BRAIN DEVELOPMENT

Bradley, M. J. & O'Connor, C. (2002). *Yes, Your Teen Is Crazy! Loving Your Kid Without Losing Your Mind*. Gig Harbor, WA: Harbor Press.

Current neurological research is now accessible to parents and teachers to help them understand the impact of brain development on teen behaviour. Because the most advanced parts of the brain are still developing throughout adolescence, teens may appear to be unpredictable and somewhat impaired in their judgment and decision-making abilities. Experimenting with alcohol and other drugs may compound these developmental "limitations." From this neurological perspective, parents need to develop appropriate expectations for adolescent behaviour that encourage them to develop internal controls and make safe choices.

About the author

David A. Wolfe, PhD, holds the inaugural RBC Chair in Children's Mental Health at the Centre for Addiction and Mental Health (CAMH). He is a Professor of Psychiatry and Psychology at the University of Toronto and Head of the CAMH Centre for Prevention Science. He is also the father of three teens.

Acknowledgments

The author acknowledges the assistance of Ms. Debbie Chiodo, M.Ed., MA, and Ms. Pat Gibbings in preparing this booklet. My colleagues Peter Jaffe, PhD, Claire Crooks, PhD, and Ray Hughes, M.Ed., contributed to the planning and purpose of this effort as part of our work on preventing adolescent risk behaviours and promoting healthy relationships (a program known as "The Fourth R" that we have been evaluating in high schools). I also thank the many parents who provided feedback and helpful suggestions so that we could make the material as relevant to them as possible.

Information for this booklet was based on research conducted in writing the book that appears below. Interested readers can consult the following source for additional information about adolescent development and risk behaviours:

Wolfe, D. A., Jaffe, P. & Crooks, C. (2006). *Adolescent Risk Behaviors: Why Teens Experiment and Strategies to Keep Them Safe.* New Haven: Yale University Press.

Reviewers

Many thanks to the following parents who formally reviewed the final draft of the manuscript: Kerry P. Clemen, Jasper Miller, Dawn Murray and Bari Zittell.

Several health care professionals and educators—most of them parents of current or past teens—also reviewed the manuscript:

David S. Goldbloom, MD, FRCPC, Senior Medical Advisor, Education and Public Affairs, CAMH

Carin McLean, BA, graduate diploma, Supervisor, Youth Outreach Service, CAMH

Cynthia Osborne, MD, Family Doctor

Cathy Stidwill, BA, B.Ed., Teacher, Ottawa-Carleton District School Board

Jo-Anne Twamley, B.A.Sc. (Family Studies), D.Ed.; Family Studies and Social Science Educator, Peel Board of Education (retired)

Siblings

...t your say but
...t necessarily their way.

fiance

Dignity / Respect + Love!

- What is the purpose of the behavior.

- Effective Parenting - teach not punish

  - Find out what "their" issue is before you start on your issue!

  - "Empathize"
    - Paraphrase back what we think they said
    - Educate yourself on a subject before you give advice.

Every Child Needs:

...veable / Capable -
Consistency